Cryptocurrency: Understanding Bitcoin, Bitcoin Cash, Ethereum & Altcoins

I0481509

Book #2 of the book series by Cryptomasher

Sean Bennett

Intro Page

Congratulations on purchasing your personal copy of *Cryptocurrency: Understanding Bitcoin, Bitcoin Cash, Ethereum & Altcoins.* Cryptocurrencies are a growing trend and have been on the rise over the past several years. There are even some online businesses that accept cryptocurrencies, such as bitcoin, as a form of payment. With the growing world of cryptocurrencies, it can seem confusing with all the options you have.

Before we dive into the logistics of cryptocurrencies, here is an overview of all the important information you will find throughout these pages:

In this book you will learn about:

- What are Cryptocurrencies
- The History of Cryptocurrencies
- Cryptocurrency and Currency
- What is Blockchain
- How to Store Cryptocurrency
- Sending and Receiving Currency
- Investing in Cryptocurrencies
- Trading Cryptocurrencies
- Virtual Profits and Actual Profits
- FOMO & FUD
- Risk Management
- ICOs

Not only will it cover the above, you will also learn:

- A Guide for Bitcoin, Bitcoin Cash, Ethererum, Litecoin & Altcoins

- The Future of Cryptocurrencies

There are endless opportunities when it comes to cryptocurrencies, so why not get involved now. They can be great investment opportunities, and they are a great way to impress your friends. Get this book today and learn the basics of the world of cryptocurrencies. Start learning more about cryptocurrency!

Enjoy the second book in the series from Cryptomasher!

Once again thank you for purchasing the book and I hope you enjoy it

Contents

Introduction

In this book, you will find information that will expand your knowledge on cryptocurrencies, such as bitcoin, and the workings behind them, such as blockchain.

Over the past several years blockchain and cryptocurrencies have grown exponentially in popularity, especially with the media. However, they are not completely free of criticism, people have tried to claim that it is only a shared database full of hype from venture capitalists, but it is actually a technology that may be able to make huge changes.

So far, blockchain, and the like, have been used as a financial service tool that improves transparency and efficiency and lowers cost. This has caused a boom in the popularity of blockchain, so much so that it is used all over the world by independent banks, innovation labs, and other entities. Many start-ups like to experiment with different ways to use this technology and try to solve some of the problems in the finance world.

The most excitement for these types of technologies can be seen in the US and Western Europe. They look at their region-specific problems when looking at how to use it. The biggest problem comes in when different entities have to learn how to collaborate with other entities. These entities can include government, commercial, and financial companies.

With the information that you will find in this book, I hope that you will have a better and deeper understanding of cryptocurrencies. Maybe with the spread of more knowledge about these amazing technologies, more people will start to use it. You will also discover that its uses span farther than financial, and it comes in handy with almost every area of business.

Thanks again for choosing this book! Every effort was made to ensure it is full of as much useful information as possible. Enjoy!

What is Cryptocurrency

This Chapter Will Cover:

- Definition of Cryptocurrency
- A Breakdown of Cryptocurrency
- Pros and Cons of Cryptocurrency

Try and look at cryptocurrencies like a digital version of a regular fiat currency, something that the government has made a legal tender, but does not have the backing of a physical commodity. But where a fiat currency used to have a link with precious mineral values, a cryptocurrency causes scarcity through the complex world of digitally solving equations or mining to make a new token.

Every different cryptocurrency has their own claims that they can solve a problem or fill a role in a better way than any other solution which came before it. The factor that unifies all cryptocurrencies is the blockchain concept, and its knack for establishing ownership and identity of record transactions and the use of the enforcing "smart contracts."

The definition of cryptocurrency, as provided by Cryptocoins News, is, "a medium of exchange like normal currencies such as USD, but designed to exchange digital information through a process made possible by certain principles of cryptography. Cryptography is used to secure the transactions and to control the creation of new coins." A different way to describe it is that cryptocurrency is a type of electricity that is converted by solving equations so that you can create digital value units that can be used a form of payment. Cryptocurrency is hard to counterfeit. The best feature of cryptocurrency is the fact that it is not issued by any main authority. Therefore, this makes it immune to any manipulation or interference by the government. Cryptocurrency is a digital currency that, instead of being printed, is mined.

At the moment, the collective value of all cryptocurrencies is around $150 to $200 billion, their numbers fluctuate a lot, and so a lot of money is involved. There are many people out there that believe this is only the beginning. As the infrastructure and technology of these coins start to grow, cryptocurrencies that can provide a real and helpful solution to different problems may end up finding their self-increasing in value rapidly, just like bitcoin did. This means investors will find them extremely attractive.

Since cryptocurrency transactions are so anonymous, this makes them suited for many illicit activities like tax evasion and money laundering.

A Breakdown of Cryptocurrency

The very first cryptocurrency to raise awareness was Bitcoin. This was launched by a group or individual that went by the alias Satoshi Nakamoto in 2009. By September 2015, there were about 14.6 million bitcoins in circulation. These held a market value of $3.4 billion. Bitcoin now has a number of competitors such as Ethereum, Namecoin, and Litecoin.

Transferring money to other people is easier with cryptocurrency. Transfers are sent by using private and public keys. These are transferred with just a small processing fee. This lets users avoid huge fees that many financial institutions and banks charge to do a wire transfer.

Pros and Cons of Cryptocurrency

The center of the genius behind cryptocurrency is the blockchains it uses to store the transactions. These transactions are stored in an online ledger. These ledgers house every transaction that has ever been made using cryptocurrencies. It gives a structure to the ledger that is not exposed to hackers, and it could be copied by any computer that runs cryptocurrency software. Experts think that blockchain has many important uses in different technologies like crowdfunding and voting. JP Morgan Chase sees cryptocurrencies as a way to lower transaction costs since it makes processing payments more efficient.

Digital cryptocurrency balances could be erased if there happened to be a computer crash and there was not a backup copy to show the holdings since cryptocurrencies are virtual and do not have a central receptacle. Prices are adjusted by supply and demand. How fast the cryptocurrency is exchanged for a different currency fluctuates greatly.

Cryptocurrencies are not immune to hacking. In Bitcoin's history, it has been subjected to at least 40 thefts that exceeded $1 million. Many look at cryptocurrencies as a currency whose value stays the same and will not fluctuate. It is easier transported than metals, facilitates exchange, and stays away from being influenced by governments and banks.

But there is a big problem. A large amount of those more than 2,000 tokens and currencies do not have a real practical use or any chance of gaining any sort of mainstream adoption. This is more than likely part of the reason why the newest trend of using these cryptocurrencies to raise money, ICOs, in China, have now been declared illegal. Many other governments, mostly in the West, have been a lot less eager to force through their regulations.

This has caused a situation a lot like the "wild west," law and order have been unable to keep pace with societal sprawl into new territories. There is a gold rush coming.

History of Cryptocurrency

This Chapter Will Cover:

- The Formative Years
- Digital Cash
- Web-Based Money

The Formative Years

Cryptocurrency has a deep and long history. The first type of cryptocurrency was created in the Netherlands during the 1980s. During the night, gas stations in remote areas were being robbed of their cash. The owners/operators did not like having to pay someone to stay there all night. The stations had to remain open so gas trucks could refuel the station during the night. Somebody had an idea of loading money on smart cards that were being tested and so we had the birth of an electronic currency. Gas delivery drivers were given these cards to carry so they would not have to worry about their cash being stolen. About this time, Albert Heijn, a very prominent retailer was trying to get his bank to find a way to let customers pay for their items out of their bank accounts. This is what is known as point-of-sale.

Before any of this happened, an American cryptographer, named David Chaum, had been trying to figure out how to make electronic cash. The way he looked at privacy and money made him think that the only way to have safe money was to have token money that would eliminate paper notes and coins. We would have the privacy of safely paying someone, and the transaction would be completely private and safe. David invented a formula in 1983. This allows people to send an amount to a person and this amount could be changed by the person who receives it. When the person who receives it, then deposits their coins, into a "bank," it keeps the original signature but is not the same number as what was signed by the mint. This allowed the coin to be changed without being traced and without breaking the mint's signature, so the mint is totally blind about the transaction.

Digital Cash

Netherland's attitude about privacy is the main reason David decided to move there. Working at CWI in the late 1980s using mathematics and cryptography research, he began DigiCash and built his vision of inventing internet money. He put it up against many names that became famous like Bryce "Zooko" Wilcox-Ahearn, Nick Szabo, Marcel "BigMac" van der Peijl, Gary Howland, Niels Ferguson, and Stefan Brands. Inventing blind cash was great as it created a huge wave of attention by the press. David along with his company made some mistakes and ended up badly with the DNB. The compromise that was agreed upon meant that the e-cash could only be sold to DNB. This caused the company to go around trying to get cash through banks. In 1998, they filed for bankruptcy. The press brought a massive amount of attention to them, including the attention of Deutsche Bank, Microsoft, and many others. Microsoft wanted him to place DigiCash on every computer that ran Windows. They were willing to pay him $180 million. David thought this was not enough money, so the deal went south, and because of this decision, DigiCash did not have any more money.

Web-Based Money

After DigiCash, there were about 100 or more startups every year working with this. In the middle 90s, attention moved from Europe to North America for two main reasons. One reason was Europe had started regulating digital cash. DigiCash had some negative reactions with a report about Prepaid Cards in 1994. The other reason was the Netscape initial public offering showed a large amount of interest in Virtual Cash. The first big wave of cryptocurrency all died out and was taken over by web-based money. First Virtual was the first to be replaced by PayPal. They both offered the same services. PayPal allowed someone to send money to anyone else. With First Merchant, you had to be a business owner to get any money. This was the same rule that regulators and banks used and was the one rule that everyone hated.

PayPal had a leap forward by being the first system to give cash from one hand to another. The first version was available on Palm Pilots. Palm Pilots were favored by the geeks. PayPal changed when they figured out that real people wanted to have money available on their web browsers. PayPal found their user base with eBay. PayPal's future was guaranteed if it stayed away from the banks and regulatory minefields that eBay put in play. PayPal proved to the web that it was the main choice for money. The tradition was still being used with Web Money in Russia.

There were also ventures that started chasing a variation of PayPal: gold via the internet. The first company to succeed in this venture was e-gold. This company was based in the Caribbean and was American-based. The idea was very simple: you gathered up your silver and gold that you no longer wanted or was broken and mailed it to them. They would then put a value on what you sent them and put "e-gold" into an account for you. You also had the option of buying new e-gold. You just wired money to a place in Florida. They, in turn, would physically buy gold and hold it for you. The founder literally hit the streets to find new customers and was able to have the company bringing in a profit by 1999. Since the e-gold issuer was offshore, it did not have to get US approval. This allowed it to target large American "goldbugs" along with other traders who needed to make cross-border payments. With this increased popularity, this type of market came to life in the year 2000.

They ran into trouble because they let anybody open an account. They began getting into a lot of scams, games, HYIPs, and ponzis and started attracting the FBI's attention. The Florida offices of e-gold were raided in 2005, and that was the end of them. The FBI also mopped up all their competitors and exchange operations they could find. This was the end of the second wave of new money.

A huge shift in the focus of new money happened on 9/11. Before this, USA was very liberal about new money. They looked at them as new businesses and innovations for the future. After the catastrophe of 9/11, their views changed drastically, but slowly. Every cryptocurrency was thought to be a hotbed for drug dealers, terrorists, and was thought to be targeted to gain control of America. It was clear that the attempts to shut down all the cryptocurrencies were going too good. Internet businesses that based themselves in America did not see any of the bad things that the government seemed to be scared of. This was when eMoney laws were put in place, but since they were Europeans, and they had not seen any evidence of what America was so scared of, they did not understand what all the hoopla was about. These barriers were what killed the deals.

Bitcoin

The domain name bitcoin.org was registered on August 18, 2008. On October 31st of the same year a link to the paper *Bitcoin: A Peer-to-Peer Electronic Cash System* that was written by Satoshi Nakamoto was posted on a mailing list to cryptographers. It detailed methods on how to use a network to generate electronic transactions without having to rely on trust. The bitcoin network came alive in January 2009 when Satoshi Nakamoto mined the first ever block of bitcoins. This is called the genesis block. It gave a reward of 50 bitcoins. Hal Finney was one of the first receivers, contributors, adopters, and supporters of Bitcoin. He downloaded the software on the day it was released and was given ten bitcoins from Nakamoto himself. This was the first every bitcoin transaction.

Cryptocurrency and Currency

This Chapter Will Cover:

- Comparing Cryptocurrency to Regular Currency
- Characteristics of Cryptocurrency
- Trading With Cryptocurrency

Cryptocurrency vs Regular Currency

Cryptocurrencies are similar to normal currencies. Its value can change along with market variables. It is used to purchase items. It has value and is recognized as a form of payment. The demand for cryptocurrency has increased within the past few years. There has been an increase in its value and circulation.

Using cryptocurrency is a lot cheaper than normal fiat currency. The need for banks decreases. You can send money to anybody around the world using cryptocurrency, and this will happen in just a matter of minutes. You do not have to stand in line at a bank and wait for it to be verified and cleared. This can take several days to complete the process. There is a nominal fee to send money whether you send $100 or $1 million. The fee is usually 0.01 percent. Cryptocurrency is a decentralized system. This means that no government owns it. Authorities do not have any power to do a thing to your account.

We have more options to become our own bank and to have complete control of our finances. Cryptocurrency has brought a new level of sophistication to new users. Some major financial institutions have begun to analyze this technology to bring it into their services.

Characteristics of Cryptocurrency

Cryptocurrency is a revolutionary system that begun with Bitcoin. All records are kept in public ledgers that can take place anywhere in the world that can transfer or receive updates and Bitcoins live. Anybody can see this at any moment and anytime. This is the innovation that Bitcoin invented and this lets it be decentralized. All cryptocurrencies come from these concepts.

Although Bitcoin was created using complex technology, cryptocurrency comes from one simple concept. Any person, anywhere in the world, from all countries and classes, could exchange credits, services, and products easily, instantly, and freely. They do not need payment gateways, merchant accounts, or banks. It is a very pure form of trade. It is the main reason the future of cryptocurrency has gained much interest and investment. In today's digital, global, and free market, cryptocurrency is holding its own as a recognized and innovative payment form.

Cryptocurrency has a base in the fundamentals of currency. Cryptocurrency goes with the characteristics of a normal pillar of traditional currency like gold. Just like gold, cryptocurrency is bound by some principles. It should be hard to find or produce. It should be in limited supply. It should be easily recognized.

Cryptocurrencies principles cannot be changed. Its technology is only able to create a certain number of cryptocurrency. The more cryptocurrency it produces, the harder it will be to make new ones. By doing this, the value gets regulated. Since it has parallels with gold, producing cryptocurrency is called mining. Computers can be bought to evaluate the complex algorithms that make the cryptocurrency. The speed that this type of computer can create cryptocurrency is determined by the speed of its processors. This type of computer is called a cryptocurrency miner.

Humans have used many different ways to trade with other things than just money. Payments have been made by bartering services or products. There are societies where people really do not need money at all. Currency does fix some problems that arise with trading in services and products. Traditional currencies do have their disadvantages. Trading internationally usually involves using many third-parties like credit card companies or banks. What these facilities provide, creates opportunities but it makes a simple exchange complicated and expensive, and it does not need to be with today's connectivity.

Cryptocurrency's purpose is to maneuver around the disadvantages of normal currencies. It gives a reliable, free, and instant way to exchange services and goods with anyone anywhere in the world. When you combine this with the principles that it was built on, cryptocurrency has become an exciting currency. Advancement in recent years and with cryptocurrency systems could evolve cryptocurrency to facilitate fast, free, and easy exchanges of services and goods.

What is Blockchain

This Chapter Will Cover:

- What is Blockchain
- The Non-Technological Explanation
- How to Understand Blockchain

Blockchain was created for one purpose. That purpose was to make an agreement for who has ownership over different balances. It is basically a tracking device.

When someone makes an online transaction like paying a person with cryptocurrency, a message gets created that has three components; a record showing proof of available funds from the buyer, the wallet's address of the recipient, and how much they are going to get paid. If there are other conditions that the buyer has specified, those are stated, and the buyer's signature is marked on the message. Digital signatures are composed of private and public code; the message gets encrypted with a code that is private and sent on for verification. The buyer's public code is what is used to decrypt the message.

This process is used so that double spend will not happen. This is a huge risk with digital currency. Double spend is when Bonnie gives Jane a dollar and then gives Dean that same dollar. This might not seem right with our current banking system, and it is true that if Bonnie were giving a true dollar to Dean and Jane, that she would not be able to double spend. With digital currency, it is just data. Anyone can edit or copy the information, and this makes it possible for anyone to give money away that they do not really have. If anyone could actually get away with doing that, it would cause a breakdown in the trust of the network.

A block will take about ten minutes to validate. This is why some buyers add tips to help speed the process up and encourage people to validate their request.

Since anybody could check a change against a ledger and get it validated, a blockchain gets rid of the need for a centralized entity like banks to manage information. By eliminating third parties, it will help save on transaction fees, processing times, and limits how large a transaction can be and to whom it may be sent.

Basically, blockchain is a database that keeps a continuously growing list of records called blocks that are secured from revisions and changes. Each block contains a timestamp and link to the block before it.

Non-Technological Explanation

Let us see if I can break this down without using all the fancy modern terms. Let us explain it like blockchain was set in pre-electricity times.

This village does not have centralized currency. They only use the barter system. The villagers get angry with how inefficient the bartering system is. They do not understand a central banking currency and worry about it. They finally decide to use a decentralized account system and write all the transactions down in a public ledger.

When someone decides to give money to someone else, they write down who they are, who the recipient is, the amount they are giving them, and the date on a piece of paper. They send it to a secure box to be written in the ledger. Keepers of the ledger then process all the submitted transactions. Several keepers must sign off on transactions before they are put into the ledger to get rid of any mistakes and fraud. With every transaction, a certain amount is put aside to give the keepers to make sure the important transactions are entered first.

When the transactions are agreed upon by all the keepers, they are written down on scrolls and then encased in glass. These are called blocks. In every block, there is a shortened version of the transaction. Every one of the blocks is chained together and put into the public archives. This makes all the transactions permanent, and the public can see them.

This is the simplest way to look at how blockchain works. It is not as complicated as some make it seem to be.

Understanding Blockchain

Blockchain technology is fairly new. This means there are many different ways to learn the system and terminology that has not been standardized yet. Blockchain works as a shared, append-only, replicated database where the access is shared with other participants, and everybody does validation.

The most common elements of blockchain are:

There is data storage that usually holds the financial transactions but really can hold any type of data. There is data replication on different systems in real time. Blockchain has a peer to peer network instead of a hierarchical model. Digital signature and cryptography is used to help prove identity, authenticity, and enforce access rights. Blockchain also has mechanisms that make it very hard to change records. If someone were to try, it is easily detectable.

Blockchains are different in how they function as to whether they are public or private. If the network is public, more security is in place than there needs to be with a private network. Blockchains have different protocols that depend on if anybody has to write them or if the participants must be limited. The blockchain's desire affects the engineering system directly. Public blockchains are more secure than private.

The blockchain is not just a file. It is a data structure. It is how data is put together logically and stored. Other types of data structures are text files; comma separated values, images, lists, and databases. A blockchain is similar to a database.

The blocks within the chain are like pages in a book. The book's pages contain a story and information about it like title, page number, and chapter. This type of data about data is referred to as meta-data.

With blockchain, every block contains the contents of a bitcoin transaction along with a header. The header is the information about the block.

Every block is then placed in an ordered fashion so that anyone will know the chain's order. For example, the pages in a book are all numbered, so if you were to rip them all out and shuffle them up, you could still put the book back in order. Just like a page, each block references back to another block with its own unique fingerprint. This fingerprint is determined by the block's content.

For a more in depth look at blockchain, see our book **'Blockchain: A Guide to Understanding Blockchain'**

Storing Cryptocurrency

This Chapter Will Cover:

- What are Wallets?

- What are Paper Wallets?

- What are Hardware Wallets?

How hard is it to choose a crypto wallet? What traits do I need to look for? This might seem like an easy answer, but it does not have a good answer. Convenience comes at the cost of security. More features could come with the cost of a harder learning curve. What traits do you value more than others? Here are some that you might want to consider:

Style: Do you get weak in the knees for new tech gadgets?

Convenience: Will I be able to purchase in a hurry if I need to?

User-friendly: Has the wallet been well designed? Is there storage for different coins?

Mobility: Is it easy to keep up with? How hard is it to lose? Can it be accessed anywhere at any time?

Security: Is the company reliable? Does it have good security?

Cost: Are there any drawbacks to using this wallet? How much does it cost?

You might want one that offers a combination of the traits listed above. Each wallet will have some advantages and disadvantages.

Wallets

A cryptocurrency wallet is a digital wallet that is used to receive, send, and store digital currency. Most cryptocurrencies have an official wallet, or some recommend third-party wallets. To use any type of cryptocurrency, you will need to have a wallet.

The cryptocurrency is not actually stored in a so-called wallet. A private key is stored that will show who owns the public key. A private key is a secure digital code that is only known by you and your wallet. A public key is a digital code that is connected to a specified amount of currency. The wallet will store your public and private keys. This lets you receive and send coins. It is also your personal ledger for transactions.

When choosing a wallet for your cryptocurrency, it is best to get one that has been endorsed by the currency you are using. If you use Bitcoin, it would be best to use the Bitcoin Core Wallet. Litecoin users should use Litecoin-QT. Ethereum users should use either MyEtherWallet or Ethereum Wallet.

There is also a universal wallet that you could use called HolyTransaction. There are offline wallets you can use if you need long-term storage called TREZOR.

If you have never used cryptocurrency, then you need to:

1. Download the official wallet from their website.
2. Sign up for a coinbase service. This will handle the exchange and wallet with one account.
3. Use a universal wallet like HolyTransaction.

If you have used cryptocurrency, there are different wallets you can choose from that have different pros and cons.

PLEASE NOTE: Some software for wallets can be disguised as malware that try to take advantage of people who are willing to download unofficial software from the internet. DO NOT trust software that is from a source that you do not know. Begin with options like the ones above, and move to different ones when you are more familiar with cryptocurrency.

PLEASE NOTE: DO NOT share your private key or password with anyone. NEVER enter your private key and password anyplace public. In order to receive or send coins, you just need to share your wallet's address or your public key.

Cryptocurrency wallets are made to be secure. The security will change with each wallet. Just like your password and username, how secure your wallet is comes from using the best practices. Do not keep more currency than you need at a time in one wallet. Use a google authenticator to get more layers of protection. Use an official wallet and encrypt your wallet. You could use multiple signature transactions as well.

It is a good idea to back up your private keys and wallet and to have them encrypted, too. Put one back up on a USB or CD to make sure you have a hard copy if needed. If you lose your keys or wallet, you will lose the currency that is connected to it.

A good rule of thumb is not to keep more money in your digital wallet than you would in a real one.

Are cryptocurrency wallets anonymous? The answer is cryptocurrency is pseudonymous. Because of the public nature and open source of blockchain ledgers, there are small bits of public data that could be used backward to find a person's identity. For many, the answer is, "it is pretty close to being anonymous."

Paper Wallets

The best way to store cryptocurrency is to use a paper wallet. By following a few simple steps, you could set one up for free. This makes you a master of your money. If you follow precautions, no one else will know your private keys. This means you need to keep a record of them.

Paper wallets are offline cold storage ways to save cryptocurrency. This means you need to print your private and public keys on paper that you will need to store in a safe place. These are printed out in QR codes that you scan when you need to access your transactions. It is safe because it gives you total control. You do not have to worry about keeping hardware running, hackers, or malware. You just need to make sure that piece of paper is safe.

Whether or not you need a paper wallet depends on your circumstances. If you are just going to take a few days during the summer to trade a few coins, them probably not. If you are in it for the long haul, and you are not planning on using any of it, then paper wallets would be the best option for you.

Paper wallets are created by using a program to generate a private and public key randomly. These keys will be unique. The program that makes them is open source. People who have advanced knowledge of coding could check the program for randomicity of the results. You are generating your key offline, and this gets rid of being exposed to online threats. If you delete the program after you use it will destroy all traces of it.

This might sound confusing, but really it is not. You do not need any specific knowledge of encryption or coding. You just need a computer, internet connection, and something to record the keys on.

To create a paper wallet, follow these steps:

1. Make sure the computer you are using is free from any malware. A new computer is ideal but is not usually feasible.

2. Go to WalletGenerator.net.

3. Download the zip file by clicking on the red word "Github."

4. When it has downloaded, open the "index.html" file. Before you do this, disconnect from the internet. This is done to ensure that the wallet is free from hackers.

5. Now, comes the time to generate your wallet. Continue to hover over the highlighted text. This will generate more characters. If you would like, you could manually type in random characters. Continue to do this until the counter gets to zero.

6. When the counter gets to zero, your wallet gets generated.

7. Print the page or make several copies of the number on it. If you print it out, make sure the printer is not connected to the internet.

8. Delete the web page. You can now reconnect to the internet.

9. Keep the private key in a long-term, secure and private place.

Hardware Wallets

These are little devices that get plugged into a phone or computer. This wallet will generate private keys safely in an environment that is offline. By generating the private keys on a device that is offline, these keys cannot be reached by hackers.

The most popular wallet is Ledger Nano S. It will cost about $70. Nano S supports Dash, Ripple, Zcash, Ethereum, Bitcoin, Litecoin, and others. These devices create private keys on a secure chip and will store them offline where they are away from hackers.

It has a screen to help you confirm and verify all outgoing transactions. This provides more security.

TREZOR is like the Nano S. This wallet was the first to have a screen. It has better security.

TREZOR will support Dash, Dogecoin, Zcash, Ethereum, Bitcoin, Litecoin, and others. It can create private keys on a secure chip. It can also store it where it cannot be connected to the internet. It costs about $99 and ships from Europe.

In order to use a hardware wallet, you must have a software wallet so you can interact with it.

All hardware wallets will have default software wallets that are made by a certain company. You could install separate software wallets to use with certain hardware wallets. An example of this is a TREZOR wallet will support Bitcoin. You could also use Electrum to use the TREZOR with Bitcoin.

You might want to do this since Electrum has unique features that TREZOR's wallets do not have such as spending from certain outputs or possibly freezing addresses so you cannot spend from them.

Sending and Receiving Cryptocurrency

This Chapter Will Cover:

- How to Receive Coins

- How to Send Coins

To receive or send cryptocurrency, you need to have a cryptocurrency wallet. The next step is to put in the recipient's and sender's address.

Most wallets will have some sort of send or request button that will facilitate a sending transaction to a certain email address or wallet. The request will serve as a way of making and seeking a payment from another address or wallet.

1. Sending is really as easy as inputting your recipient's email address into the correct fields.

2. The next tab will then have you specify the amount of coin that you want to send.

3. The third step will have you specify the account from which you want to have the payment deducted.

4. After you have hit the send button, your transaction will be complete.

The recipient will be about to the see the incoming amount show up in their wallet. The sender's balance will also then reflect the deduction of the amount they transferred. On a bitcoin network, it will take about an hour for everything to be confirmed and approved as a legitimate transaction.

You need to exercise extreme caution when you are sending and receiving cryptocurrencies. After a transaction has been initiated most protocols will not allow you to cancel them. Therefore, you have to make sure that you want to send the coin, and send to the right address before you ever start activating the send button. However, the sender does have the option of asking the recipient for a refund of the amount that they sent. These types of transactions are anchored on the agreement of both of the parties.

One of the most important parts of your wallet is the key address. This address is what you use for sending and receiving coins. Nearly all cryptocurrency address are going to look similar to 1KDCn9XLVu3xNyr7ox64yjLw3kvKM1bADM.

You should view this as a bank account number. These strings are also able to be represented via QR-codes. QR-codes are widely used when it comes to mobile wallets for more convenience. All cryptocurrency transactions have their own unique transaction IDs and cannot be reversed. After you have sent the money to another person, there is no way of undoing it.

For a transaction to be considered valid, it has to be validated by the network. This is what is known as 'confirmation.' A confirmation could take as long as a couple of seconds to several minutes, depending on how much load is going through the network.

For every transaction, a user will have to pay a small fee. This fee may range from less than a cent to up to a few cents, and maybe even as much as a dollar, and this fee will automatically be subtracted from your balance.

A lot of wallets will offer you the opportunity to see how many bitcoins you have as USD or EUR equivalent. This will allow you to type in the amount of USD or EUR you want to send out to another user, and the wallet will then be able to automatically calculate the amount of coin that will be needed for that transaction.

You can even follow your transaction. To do so, you can paste the transaction ID into the search box. The transaction IDs are unique for every single transaction, and you will see them in your wallet. Another way to follow a transaction to or from an address is to paste the address into your search box. This will show you all incoming and outgoing transactions associated with that address.

The process of receiving and sending cryptocurrencies such as Ether, Litecoin, Bitcoin, etc. will differ with each wallet since each coin has its own options that the cryptocurrency could be stored in. In general, these are the steps you would use:

1. You need to log into your wallet.

2. Click on the button or tab that says "send/receive."

3. Choose if you are going to receive or send cryptocurrency. You can only receive or send coins that are alike. For example, you are only allowed to receive or send Litecoin to Litecoin, Bitcoin to Bitcoin. You are not able to send Ethereum to a Bitcoin wallet.

4. **To send:** Enter the public wallet address of the person you are sending money to and put in the amount you are sending. Make sure you have enough money in the wallet to pay for the fees plus the amount being sent. Double and triple check the numbers, to make sure you are not making any mistakes. When you have verified everything, hit "send transaction." Check the transaction one more time to make sure you have the addresses correct. You can add notes to the transaction to let the person you are sending it to know what it is for.

5. **To receive:** You really do not have to do anything except give the sender your public wallet address. If you are with them, you can let them scan your QR code if your wallet allows this.

If you are still not sure, look at the FAQ for your wallet to make sure you are doing the right steps.

QUICK TIP: You can use Shapeshift to turn one cryptocurrency into a different one. This is very helpful if you use Bitcoin, but need to send someone money who uses Ethereum.

PLEASE NOTE: Do not ever give anyone your private key. Sharing a public address is not a problem. Share your public address. The only thing that could happen is somebody adds money to it. DO NOT ever share your private keys or password. This is like giving a complete stranger your bank account information.

There are bitcoin ATMs in public places that give people the chance to purchase bitcoins with cash. You will have to make sure to install a wallet first to be able to transfer the coins to an address that you want.

There are also gift cards and voucher cards that can be used. Voucher cards may be available in stores in your area. These will look a lot like any other gift card, and you can redeem them online. These are great options for small online purchases.

Cryptocurrency Investing

This Chapter Will Cover:

- How to Invest in Cryptocurrency.
- Which Ones to Invest in.
- Where Can You Get Them.
- Do You Need to Pay Tax on Them?

You may be thinking about investing in cryptocurrency. Cryptocurrencies are the hottest investment around right now. These exchangeable tokens promise to be the new money for the entire world. These people see a future where cryptocurrencies will take the place of the dollar, the Mexican peso, British pound, or the Euro. They want to create the first free world currency.

Having Bitcoin means you own a share of this venture. If Bitcoin were ever to replace monetary reserves or become the main currency for world trade, its value would be well beyond 100,000 USD. By buying and keeping cryptocurrencies is betting on the success of this new money revolution.

Cryptocurrecy investing is essentially buying some coin and holding onto that coin in the hope that the value of that coin will go up. For example, if you were to buy Litecoin (LTC) when its price was $50 per coin and you hold onto that coin for two years and sell it for $250 a coin you essentially invested for two years to make a 400% profit. Similarly, if you to buy that same coin at $250 and sold at $50 you would have made a loss of 400%. It is however noteworthy that all cryptocurrencies which have a strong user base have only risen in the long run.

Yes, it would have been in your best interest to invest years ago. However, it is not too late. If you understand the potential that can be found and if you believe in this vision, today is a good day to invest in cryptocurrency.

Crypto Investments

Cryptocurrencies are not normal investments. There volatility greatly exceeds any other class of investments. They are unregulated. There is a potential risk that they will get outlawed. They might be someone out there who learns how to hack into them. You could also lose your key. Investing in cryptocurrencies is very high risk. It is important to realize that you should only invest as much as you can stand to lose. Do not invest everything you own. Only invest in what you can afford to lose if it all goes away tomorrow.

There are three main reasons to invest in cryptocurrencies:

- You want to increase your net worth encase the Dollar falls. Many people assume this will eventually happen.

- You support cryptocurrency's vision that the entire world needs a free money.

- You like the technology and understand it.

There are also bad reasons to invest in cryptocurrencies. Many will fall victim to all the hype around each cryptocurrency. There will always be someone who gets captured by the fear of missing out (FOMO). They will buy huge amounts at the peak hoping to make fast money. They do not understand it. This is a very bad reason. You need to learn about your investments.

Bitcoin was the only cryptocurrency for a time. That is up until the late part of 2016. If you wanted to invest in cryptocurrency, you had to buy Bitcoin. Other cryptocurrencies were called Altcoins, they were just penny stocks on shady markets just to keep miner's GPUs working. They would just up the price then dump the coins.

This has all changed. Bitcoin is still the main cryptocurrency, but in 2017, its shares fell from 90 to about 40 percent. Many saw this as a result of Ethereum's growing popularity. Bitcoin's community is having issues with the size of the blocks. This shows why it is important to keep your ears and eyes open to what the cryptocurrency community is saying.

If you still want to invest, Bitcoin is still the main one in everyone's portfolio, but it is not the ONLY asset. In every well-balanced portfolio you might find coins like:

- Monero
- Dashcoin
- Litecoin
- Ripple
- Ethereum
- And many more (to be explained)

If you want a balanced portfolio, it is good just to reflect the ten most valuable cryptocurrencies within your portfolio. You need to take the time and read about these coins and decide if you agree with their vision and use it to choose your selections.

Crypto Exchanges

Some coins focus more on privacy such as Zcash, Monero, and Dash. Some focus on smart contracting such as Ethereum. Some use scaling payments such as Dashcoin and Litecoin. Bitshares, Nem, and Ripple are decentralized and less open to Bitcoin and others.

The cryptocurrency market is blazing. It is a confusing system where you could find many chances to get a lot of money or possibly lose it. Each day gives birth to new cryptocurrencies and death to old ones. Each day some coins fall heavily, and some rise vertically.

If you choose to buy altcoins, there are some ways to find the good ones from the bad. Good coins will have a clear technical vision, and active team, and an enthusiastic, vivid community. Bad coins are not clear, they do not have any technical advantages, and you will never be able to reach them. Their community is only focused on making more money. The worst cryptocurrencies are MLM coins like OneCoin. They target the uninformed with a marketing system that has many different levels, and they promise they are going to be the new Bitcoin. Stay away from them.

Years ago it was hard to buy cryptocurrencies; now you have many different options.

Let us look at buying Bitcoin. This is the easy part. Some want to invest without having to go through the problems of storing them.

You could use investment strategies such as XBT tracker, Second Markets, Bitcoin ETI, etc. XBT tracker is available to German and Swedish exchanges. Second Markets is for USD. Bitcoin ETI is used in Germany and Gibraltar. The more Bitcoin rises, the more brokers are trying to set up financial products based on Bitcoin.

These investment products enable investors to bet on Bitcoin's price without buying Bitcoin. Many fans of cryptocurrency think this gets rid of the fun of it. Many people think it is the easiest way to invest in Bitcoin. You could use what you already use to invest, and if anything were to go wrong, you can take your certificate to court and sue someone.

If you would like to own real Bitcoins or you just want to stay away from paying the high fees for investing, you can buy Bitcoin directly. You have options for buying anywhere in the world. In Europe, you could use Kraken or Bitcoin.de. In America, you could use Gemini, BitStamp, BitFinex, or Coinbase. In Asia, there is BitFlyer, BTCChina, and OKCoin.

Buying Bitcoin is not a problem. You just open an account with the exchange, verify your identity, and fund the account with USD, Euro, or the paper money your country uses. On Bitcoin.de you do not need to fund the account, you just trade with other users.

The exchange you use all depends on where you live. It is always better to use one that is close to you. If it is located within your jurisdiction, you have better chances of legally getting your money back if something were to go wrong. If there is not an exchange in your jurisdiction, use one that is based in a stable country that has a good legal system.

One more factor is which exchange will use the coins you want to invest in and how much patience you have. If you are looking to acquire a large amount of Bitcoin very quickly, you should use a major exchange that gives the liquidity you need. If you are only wanting a small amount of coins and are not in a hurry to make millions, you can buy them on smaller exchanges. If you can get your order filled, you will get a better price than using a larger exchange.

Altcoins are harder to buy than Bitcoin. Major exchanges such as BitStamo, BitFinex, and Kraken have begun to list popular Altcoins such as Ripple, Monero, Ethereum, and Litecoin. If these are part of your portfolio, try to find a one-stop shop that deals with all of them.

There are hundreds of different cryptocurrencies available. If you want a crypto supermarket, a place where you can sell and buy most of them, then register at an altcoin exchange.

For example:

- Poloniex
- Bithumb
- Yunbi
- Bittrex

The website coinmarketcap is very useful because it will list every crypto exchange. It sorts them by trade volume.

The Altcoin exchanges do not have strict know your customer (KYC) rules since you are not trading with fiat money. You can fund the account with Bitcoin. This will serve as an account for all altcoin markets, just like a USD works with Forex markets.

With Bitcoin exchanges, you need to choose one that many people trust. Most altcoin exchanges are not regulated, most of these are located in Asia. Do not ever place a lot of trust in these. You will not be able to get any money back if they file for bankruptcy or get hacked. Bittrex and Poloniex are US based and provide a safe and secure trading environment.

There is no true rule of when to buy. It is not a good idea to purchase at the peak, and it is not smart to buy when it is crashing. It is never wise to catch a knife that is falling. The best time is when the price is stable and low.

Decide when the cryptocurrency you want to buy is in bubble mode and has reached the bottom after it has fallen. There is never an absolute certainty to anything. A coin might begin to rise, and once it has passed a mark, and everyone thinks this is the peak, the rally is just beginning.

There are two pieces of advice to follow:

1. Do not try to compare crypto bubbles with normal financial bubbles. Ten percent means it is up, but it does not mean it is a bubble. It might just be the daily volatility. It might be a bubble when it gets to 100 percent, but most of the time it is just the beginning. It is definitely a bubble at 1,000 percent, but there is not a guarantee that it is going to pop.

2. Just watch. Do not buy just because you saw a dip. There could be another one. Do not buy in just because it is going to explode tomorrow. Just watch, be informed, and buy when you think the time is right. Most importantly, do not be weak. Do not sell early. Hold on to it. Its value has just begun.

Crypto Tax

DISCLAIMER: This is in no way tax advice. If you have questions about taxes or if there is a lot of money involved, please talk to a local tax consultant.

There are only a handful of tax consultants that know about cryptocurrencies. The number is growing, and soon cryptocurrencies are going to be standard for most tax experts just like real estate, ETFs, shares, and securities.

This is just giving you an overview of normal issues with taxes and cryptocurrencies.

Nothing is for certain other than taxes and death. This goes for cryptocurrencies, too. If you get money from investing in cryptocurrencies, you will likely have to pay taxes on it just like money made from regular income from a job or other investments.

The way you need to tax your cryptocurrency returns is up to your tax jurisdiction.

There is good news about taxes and cryptocurrencies. Almost every country in the world is value-added tax exempt when dealing with cryptocurrencies. With each financial product, you do not have to pay value-added tax when you sell Bitcoin. Some tax authorities in Sweden, Germany, Estonia, and Poland demanded value-added tax when you sell cryptocurrency. When the European Court stopped this, VAT on Bitcoins seems to be not a concern anymore.

In many jurisdictions, you do not have to pay any taxes. Germany is known for its very high taxes, but is now a tax haven for cryptocurrencies. Just like American and other countries, Germany thinks Bitcoin is not a financial product but a property. If you make money when you trade it, you do not have to pay a flat tax on income. This is usually around 25 percent. For interest on bank accounts, you must pay the tax on the profit when selling and buying cryptocurrencies just like income.

You do have a loophole. If you can hold onto your coins for over one year, you do not have to pay taxes on them when you decide to sell them. This rule got added to try to de-incentivize day trading and to stabilize the price by giving holders incentives. The Netherlands and Germany became a tax haven for cryptocurrencies. Other countries have similar rules. If you are ever in doubt, ask a tax advisor.

There is one problem the one year rule causes. You must prove you have held the cryptocurrency for this amount of time. Exchanges will help you print out your trade history. You could also use the blockchain to prove storage. With most cryptocurrencies, it is clear when coins are spent or received.

If you use an exchange to track your trades, taxing Bitcoin is possible, it also causes a lot of problems. You must calculate every profit and not just the ones from trading but from Bitcoins if you use it to pay for things.

Things get extremely complicated when talking about Altcoins. For many tax authorities, Altcoins are treated like Bitcoins. In many countries, they look at it as a property instead of a financial product. If you buy with Bitcoin and sell it for Bitcoin, you need to tax the difference but not in Bitcoin but in actual money. You have to keep track of all the cryptocurrency trading as well as the price of Bitcoin when buying and selling.

This makes everything complicated. You might have bad trades, and this could result in getting fewer Bitcoins than you originally invested. This means you are still accountable for taxes if the price of Bitcoin soared between trades. You lost money in a trade, but you are still responsible for paying the taxes on it.

You need to accept the fact that cryptocurrency is something new. You are not an expert when dealing with financial authorities. Ask your local tax advisor for a consultation. Talk to them about cryptocurrencies and enjoy watching their confused faces trying to answer your questions.

Above all, enjoy investing in cryptocurrencies.

Cryptocurrency Trading

This Chapter Will Cover:

- Different Types of Crypto Trading
- What You Need to Do Before You Begin Trading.
- What You Should Know to Begin Trading.
- How to Start Trading.

Cryptocurrency trading is different type of making money than cryptocurrency investing. Cryptocurrency investing is a long term investment while cryptocurrency trading is a short term way of making money. It is very lucrative if you play your cards right.

There are two main ways of trading which will briefly be covered in this book. I will be releasing another book with a number of strategies and tips in the near future. The first is traditional buy low, sell high or 'buying long'. The other way is 'short trading' or 'shorting', when a trader buys high and sells low.

Buying Long

Buying long is the most well-known way of trading. It is the same as if you trade goods or services. If you buy say five coin of Monero (XMR) in the morning at a price of $200 a coin. The long trader's goal would be to sell that hand at a price higher than $200. If in the evening the price of Monero went up to $230 and you sold your whole stake you would have made $150 profit minus platform fees, or a 15% profit. It is really quite simple. It is buying for a low price and selling it at a higher price.

Short Trading

Above you may have been thinking how can someone buy high and sell low and still make a profit? This is a question which always comes up when explaining trading to the uninitiated. One must be very careful with shorting and I only advise it for people who have had at least a few long trades under their belt.

Short trading is when one of the trading platforms allow the trader to borrow a certain amount of coin from them and the trader leverages on the price of that coin dropping in price. The following example should make it simple. A trader would for example borrow two coin of Bitcoin Cash (BCC) from the trading platform at $1800 and sell it at that price. The trader would then bet on the coin falling in price. When the trader sees that the value of Bitcoin Cash has dropped to $1650 dollars the trader would then buy two coins and pay the platform back their two coins of BCC. That would leave the trader with a profit of $300 or about 9%. The trader did not borrow $1800 to pay it back at $1650 to make a loss, they borrowed two coins and payed back two coins and kept the difference in dollars.

Get Started With Cryptocurrency Trading

To be able to trade cryptocurrency there are a few things you must do before you can begin. You must have a wallet and choose an exchange.

After this, you just need to fill out some forms and wait for the transaction to go through. The exchange you choose has to verify your information.

We have already discussed how to invest in cryptocurrency, so you probably have some of these in a wallet. An exchange-broker-wallet like GDAX or Coinbase allows you to sell and buy actual cryptocurrency.

There are just a few things you need to know about trading cryptocurrency.

Some of the more important ones are:

- A cryptocurrency exchange is not involved with the regular stock exchange.

- If you are just starting out, you might want to trade cryptocurrency stocks on the normal stock market. GBTC is one that owns Bitcoin and sells shares of it. By trading on this, you stay away from trading cryptocurrency directly. Stock transactions are faster than normal cryptocurrency transactions.

- The easiest place to trade cryptocurrency is Coinbase. You are only allowed to trade Litecoin, Ethereum, and Bitcoin on Coinbase. If you seriously want to trade cryptocurrency, you need another exchange like Coinbase's Kraken, Binance, Bittrex, or GDAX.

- The market for cryptocurrency is incredibly volatile. You could make a fortune in a second or lose it all. It does not matter if you trade Bitcoin, other cryptocurrencies, or on the GBTC Bitcoin trust. Think about taking risks, hedging, and do not go along with your funds.

You can choose any exchange, but GDAX and Coinbase is the best places to start because they are easy to use.

There are several sides to cryptocurrency:

1. You can invest and trade it.
2. You can use it to buy things.
3. You can use a graphics processing unit along with some software and mine coins.

If you are a beginner, begin by choosing a company who has a good reputation and that offers both a wallet and exchange. You need to begin by trading prominent cryptocurrency like Ethereum, Litecoin, and Bitcoin. This might change in the future.

Coinbase is the most popular cryptocurrency website in America. It offers one platform for wallet that supports Litecoin, Ethereum, and Bitcoin.

Once you have mastered coinbase, you are now ready to try GDAX or other exchanges like Kraken, Binance, or Bittrex.

Here are the steps you need to take to trade on coinbase:

1. Sign up for a coinbase account and create a wallet where you will store your digital currency.

2. Connect your credit card, debit card, and bank account so you can exchange digital currency in and out of your local currency.

3. Buy Litecoin, Ethereum, or Bitcoin. You are basically trading USD for cryptocurrency.

4. Think about signing up for a different exchange and trade cryptocurrency for cryptocurrency. Then you can transfer that back to Litecoin, Ethereum, or Bitcoin. Then back into coinbase and back into dollars. Remember to record your transactions for tax purposes.

Coinbase wants a lot of personal information that you will not feel comfortable with giving. You have to do this. The more information that you can give them, the higher your limit will be, and your account will not be restricted.

It is best to use a bank account and do not use credit or debit cards. The fees will be a lot lower with a bank account. The fees are higher without one.

You will have to input your bank account login when you sign into your bank account. This might feel shady, but it is all part of the process.

When using your bank account, you will have to wait between three and five days for the bank to approve. You will not be able to trade for about one week.

There will be limits on how much you can sell or buy in one week. Add a photo identification along with other payment methods will increase your limit. Your limit will increase fast with time the more you trade.

There are going to be fees involved when trading. They will go down the more you trade. Different exchanges do have better rates like GDAX. You will pay a bit more over market price or sell a bit lower than market price and pay small fees when you trade on coinbase.

Set up a two-step authentication. This will help you secure your account by sending your phone a code when you log in.

To trade coins, you will have to go into settings, and your wallets need to be set up.

The benefit of having a USD wallet on coinbase is you can put money into it and buy coins from the wallet. If you try to buy with your bank account, it will take about one week. Using a credit card does not create this problem but will the limit will be less.

You can buy fractions of coins. Bitcoins are expensive so think about just buying a fraction of a coin, to begin with if you do not have much money to start-up capital. It is a mistake to buy just Litecoin or Ethereum because Bitcoin is more expensive. You need to know which one is going to increase and retain its value. Buying all three in equal increments is a good way to stay away from making the wrong choice just based on price per coin.

When you purchase a coin, review the information. One extra decimal point might mean big money when you consider one Bitcoin can trade for tens of thousands of dollars.

Downloading the app on your phone will let you trade with your phone. The market can be volatile, and the transaction is slow. You need to be about to sell or buy as quickly as possible.

Set up alerts to help you know when you need to sell or buy.

You can buy increments with time. Coinbase will automate this feature for you.

Cryptocurrency can be volatile. There will always be a chance that the market might crash. You could also face other catastrophes. Cryptocurrencies are not a regulated fiat currency or centrally controlled. If you lose your coins or somebody cheats you out of them, there is not anything you can do.

Trading cryptocurrency is simple, to begin with, but there are aspects you need to understand before you begin with an exchange like coinbase.

There are many options to set up wallets and trading currency. Many will pair with a coinbase account thus making it a great place to start.

Cryptocurrency Exchanges

One of the best ways for you to start buying coins is to open up a wallet with one of the big cryptocurrency exchange websites. To get an account, every user will need to provide official document ID. Once you are part of the exchange, you will be able to buy most of the popular coins and then hold part of them in the same wallet.

This is a convenient way to get coins and will help save you so much time. This is known as an online wallet, and people will often rely on the exchange to help keep their funds safe. After you have purchased your first bitcoin or any other type of cryptocurrency, you need to consider transferring these funds to a more secure wallet, unless you are planning on using them for investing and trading. The secured wallet needs to be controlled by you, and only you. There are many different ways that you can purchase cryptocurrency. For a bit of simplicity, we will look at exchanges that provide you with Bitcoin.

1. **Coinbase** – this probably the most popular online exchange for Bitcoin in the US. It also operates in several European countries and helps to provide the best in class user experience and usability. This is one of the very few exchanges that insure all of the funds that are stored on their platform. In the case of a security breach, their insurance policy will help to cover all losses. They also have a mobile app that you can use. You can buy Bitcoin with the use of a credit card or bank wire.

   Use the like below to buy $100 worth of coin and receive $10 free.

2. **Anycoindirect** – this is a European cryptocurrency exchange. This exchange does not provide you with a dedicated online wallet. Customers can use their bank account to send money to the provider. Once the money has been received, users will get the number of Bitcoins transferred to the address that they originally provided.

3. **Cex** – this exchange allows for buying bitcoins with bank transfers and credit card. This exchange provides worldwide coverage and has a trading platform with the ability for margin trading.

4. **Shapeshift** – this is a different type of exchange. This platform is aimed towards users that have a portfolio of different cryptocurrencies. The idea behind this is to easily swap out one type of coin for another coin, without the need to register for an account. This platform offers a great level of privacy. If you already have your own bitcoins, this is the perfect place to purchase other cryptocurrencies.

5. **LocalBitcoins** – this is a P2P Bitcoin exchange. Sellers and buyers will agree to certain trade terms. The exchange will connect local people who want to trade bitcoins. The payment methods will be determined by the sellers. You can purchase coins using PayPal, through bank, or cash. This platform can offer a very high level of privacy.

6. **Kraken** – this is a US based cryptocurrency trading and exchange platform. This exchange also operates in Europe. On this exchange, you can margin trade. You can only buy bitcoins on Kraken with bank transfers.

7. **Bitrush** – this is a cryptocurrency exchange that operates in Europe. People can purchase coins instantly through a credit card, MyBank, Bancontact, and iDEAL

8. **Bitstamp** – this is the first licensed and regulated virtual currency exchange in the EU. Users can deposit funds using bank transfers and then purchase bitcoins. This exchange also works as a trading platform.

9. **Gemini** – this is a cryptocurrency trading platform and exchange. This exchange only operates in the US at the moment. It allows for both institutional and individual customers to store, buy, and sell assets. Additionally, the platform FDIC insures up to $250,000 per beneficial owner. You can purchase bitcoins with a bank deposit.

10. **OkCoin** – this is one of the largest Chinese trading platforms and exchanges.

11. **Coinmama** – this is a bitcoin broker that specializes in allowing users to purchase bitcoin with a credit card or a debit card.

FOMO & FUD

This Chapter Will Cover:

- What is FUD

- What is FOMO

- The meaning behind many cryptocurrency lingo words

There is a long list of cryptocurrency lingo that can be daunting at best. Let us look at some of the most common acronyms that you may come across when you start working in cryptocurrencies.

1. **HODL** – this was originally a misspelling of the word hold, but it stuck around to mean keep. A trader who buys coins and does not see themselves selling in the near future is known as a HODLER of the coin.

2. **FOMO** – this acronym stands for the 'Fear of Missing Out.' This is the feeling you get when you see a large green candle on a chart, and you do not own any of that coin, so you end up selling other stuff to buy into it. Since crypto trading is still very emotionally driven, instead of value-driven, FOMO is a huge factor to consider when a person swings trades in crypto.

3. **FUD** – this is an acronym that stands for 'fear, uncertainty, and doubt.' This is normally used in a statement like "xxx spreading FUD again." A real world of example of FUD is when JPMorgan's Dimon spread FUD by saying that Bitcoin was only a fraud that will eventually blow up.

4. **ATH** – this is the short form of 'all-time high.' This means that the coin is at its highest historical price.

5. **Whale** – this describes a huge player who has a decent amount of capital. Whales are also often the market movers for the small altcoins because of their huge capital.

6. **Pump and Dump** – this is the recurring cycle of an altcoin receiving a spike in its price which is followed by a crash. These types of movements are often attributed to low volume, hence the word pump. Traders that choose to pump, buy large amounts, may want to cause the uninformed investors to experience FOMO, and then dump or sell their coins at a better price.

7. **Shill** – this is the act of unsolicited endorsement of a coin to the public. Traders who have bought a coin may have an interest in shill the coin in the hopes of igniting some interest in the coin.

8. **Bag holder** – this is used to refer to a trader who bought at a high and then missed their chance to sell, leaving them with worthless coins.

9. **Margin Trading** – this refers to trading with leverage. When this happens, you have borrowed one side of the trading pair at a certain loan rate and then sell it for the other side. Depending on how you think the market will move, you could place a long or short bet on a pair.

10. **Long** – this is a position that a trader takes. A long position believes that its value will go up in the future.

11. **Short** – this is a position that a trader takes. A short position believes that its value will go down in the future.

12. **Fill or Kill** – this is a limit order that will not execute unless an opposite order goes past this limit order amount.

13. **Weak Hands** – this refers to people who are not patient and sell at loss whenever the market goes down.

Risk Management

This Chapter Will Cover:

- How to reduce risk in cryptocurrency trading
- The importance of the news
- Dollar Cost Averaging

As you have probably seen, the price for cryptocurrencies tends to fluctuate wildly in a given week. Right now things may seem fairly good, but chances are, two weeks ago most of the currencies were in the red.

Considering that cryptocurrencies are still fairly new, there are going to be some periods of change. The news will heavily influence how the market views things, and with the different incidents that happen with cryptocurrencies, it makes sense that most people will consider selling off. These dips and crashes are risks that you cannot avoid; however, you can mitigate them.

Make sure that you keep up with the news. The news can either make or break your possible profits. Some great websites for up-to-date news on cryptocurrencies are cryptocoinsnews.com and altcointoday.com. It is also a good idea to keep an eye on the personal websites of the coins that you invest in.

No matter what things you invest in, there are going to be some risks associated with it. When you choose to invest in cryptocurrencies, you take the chance that the coin may crash or lose value. You should not invest all of your money into a coin. Remember what the Billionaire J.R. Simplot said, "never spend your taw." This means that you should never spend what need in order to continue playing the investment game.

But whenever you have a risk, there is an opportunity. People invest in cryptocurrencies because they believe that the value will go up and overall there has been some impressive growth across the board over the last few months. This will help to reduce the risk of investing because you can see the crashes and dips that have happened before, and, for the most part, the mark tends to recover as well as surge ahead in value.

One dip in Ethereum, it went from 250 to 130, and then it rose to 400. Anybody that bought into Ethereum when it was at the 130 mark would still be way up on their return even with a dip.

Timing is also very important. If you think that investing in cryptocurrencies is going to be a get rich quick scheme for you, you will probably end up sorely disappointed. Just because you notice a currency jump up 400% a month ago does not mean that it is going to do that again. You have to make sure you watch the market, and it will take some time.

There are plenty of Bitcoin millionaires out there. The thing that made them rich more than anything else was being patient, and letting time run its course. They bought into bitcoin when it was pretty much worthless and held onto their shares for years until now, when it is worth thousands of dollars.

So when you buy some coins, make sure you consider holding onto them and allowing them to mature with some time before you choose to sell them. Make sure that you are not quick to sell off your coins when you notice a dip. This is a good way to end up losing money. Wait till the market has time to swing back up.

Dollar Cost Averaging

A Good way to protect yourself when investing is to buy a set number of coin at a certain interval on a regular basis. This will protect you from the major swings that occur with cryptocurrency. Of course, while traders make their money on the price swings, long term investors will end up with a overall percentage protection when using dollar cost averaging. If you were to purchase Ethereum every week, and over a months period you purchased the coin three weeks at where the price of the coin was low and one week you purchased when it was high, you have had managed your risk of buying all your coin in that week when the price was high.   With dollar cost averaging you have come out on top.

The biggest thing you need to make sure you do, and I cannot stress this enough, is to make sure that you back up your wallets. There are so many horror stories out there of people who end up losing the computer or wallet, and they no longer can access their coins. Print you backup phrases and out and lock them up in a safe place.

ICOs

This Chapter Will Cover:

- What are ICOs
- How ICOs can be dangerous
- How they are used in cryptocurrency

The definition of ICOs, Initial Coin Offering, is an unregulated way that funds are raised for a new cryptocurrency venture. ICOs are often used by startups to bypass the regulated and rigorous capital-raising process that is required by venture capitalists or banks. In a campaign, a percentage of a cryptocurrency is sold to all the early backers for the project in exchange for another cryptocurrency or legal tender, but usually for Bitcoin.

When a startup cryptocurrency is interested in raising money with an ICO, it will come up with a plan on paper that will tell what the project will be about, what they will do once finished, how much money they will need, how many virtual tokens the pioneers will keep, what money they accept, and the length of their campaign.

Roger Bryan, the founder of Digital Currency Index, believes that more control needs to be in place before cryptocurrency markets being to attract institutional investments that many of these projects need to hit their complete potential.

Right now, people who are interested in staking a claim in future currencies with the use of blockchain, token, or project can achieve this by using many ICOs. This could end up requiring a $10,000 buy-in or more.

Bitcoin tends to be a gatekeeper, which means you need bitcoin to invest with different cryptocurrencies. This is one of the most common uses for this type of currency, and it is one that has played a huge role in the rise of its value.

During a campaign, people who support the initiative will buy some coins that have been distributed with regular currency or cryptocurrency. These are called tokens and are similar to company shares that are sold to investors in IPO transactions. They do not raise the number of funds they need, the money is given back to the bankers, and the ICO is seen as unsuccessful. If they do meet the fund's requirement in time, the money that gets raised will start a new scheme or complete the other one.

Investors are excited to buy coins hoping that their plan will be successful once it is launched. This might give a higher value than what was originally paid for it. The smart contract platform, Ethereum, is an example of an ICO project that has been very successful.

ICOs work similarly to crowdfunding and IPOs. Like an IPO, a stake in the company or startup is sold to raise some money for the operations during the ICO. IPOs are deals with investors, ICOs are deals with supporters. An ICO differs from crowdfunding in that the backers are motivated by a possible return on their investment, while crowdfunding funds are donations.

Even though there are some successful ICO transactions, ICOs are more poised to be disruptive, innovative tools. Investors should be cautious as some ICOs or crowd sales are fraudulent. Since these fundraising operatives are not regulated in any way by financial authorities, like the Securities Exchange Commission, funds that an investor loses because of fraudulent initiatives may not be recovered.

The People's Bank of China, in early September 2017, officially banned ICOs. They cited it was disrupting the stability of the economy. The central bank did not want the tokens to be used as currency on the market and banks could not offer any services that were related to ICOs. As a result, Ethereum and bitcoin tumbled, and it was seen as a sign that regulations surrounding cryptocurrencies are nigh.

A Guide to Cryptocurrency

This Chapter Will Cover:

- The workings of various cryptocurrencies

- How various cryptocurrencies work

- How various cryptocurrencies compare

Bitcoin BTC

Bitcoin was created by an anonymous person known as Satoshi Nakamoto in 2009. All transactions are void of middlemen, which mean no banks. People can use Bitcoin to book hotel rooms on Expedia, shop on Overstock, and buy Xbox games. But most people use it to 'get rich' by trading it. In 2017, the price of Bitcoin shot up into the thousands.

People can use Bitcoin to buy merchandise anonymously. International payments are also easier and cheaper with Bitcoin because they are not tied to certain countries or subject to regulation. Small businesses often like Bitcoin because they do not have to worry about credit card fees. There are some people that only buy Bitcoins as an investment in the hopes that they will go up in value.

Marketplaces known as 'Bitcoin exchanges' give people the chance to buy and sell Bitcoins with different currencies. Coinbase is one of the most popular exchanges. People can also send Bitcoins to other people with computers or mobile apps. People can compete to 'mine' Bitcoins by solving complex math puzzles. Winners are rewarded with a number Bitcoins every ten minutes.

All Bitcoin transactions are recorded in a public loop, but the names of the sellers and buyers are never revealed, only their wallet IDs. While this helps to keep users' transactions private, it also gives them the change to buy or sell whatever they want without easily tracing it back to them.

Bitcoin Cash BCH/BCC

Bitcoin cash was created in August 2017 as a fork of Bitcoin classic. With Bitcoin Cash, they increased the size of the blocks, which allows more transactions to be processed.

Ever since Bitcoin started, they have faced pressure from members when it comes to scalability. Specifically, the size of the blocks, 1 megabyte or 1,024 kilobytes in 2010, would slow the transaction process time down, thus limiting the potential of the currency. Block size limit was written into the code to stop potential spam attacks when Bitcoin's value was low. Bitcoin's popularity increased greatly by 2015, and the average block size was around 600 bytes. That created the chance of transaction times running into delays as more blocks started to reach their max capacity.

Many ideas have been tried to handle processing the transactions with time. Most of the focus has been on increasing the block size. Since the code for Bitcoin is not handled by a central entity, changes that need to be made require a buy-in from miners and developers. This means that proposals can take some time to be finished. This caused groups to make different blockchain ledgers with new standards, known as a fork. Many forks, like Bitcoin Unlimited and Bitcoin XT, failed to be adopted. Thus Bitcoin Cash launched in August 2017.

Bitcoin Cash increases the block size from 1 MB to 8 MB. It also got rid of Segregated Witness or SegWit. This is a proposed code adjustment that will free up block space by getting rid of parts of the transaction. The goal for Bitcoin Cash is to increase how many transactions can be processed. The supporters behind it hope that the change will allow Bitcoin Cash to compete with the amount of transactions which can be handled by PayPal and Visa.

Since the amount of computer power to process the bigger blocks could price out the smaller miners, critics are worried that Bitcoin Cash could lead to power being concentrated with companies that can afford better equipment.

Use the like below to buy $100 worth of coin and receive $10 free.

https://www.coinbase.com/join/582759ff21649a5de502ef18

Bitcoin Gold BTG

Another fork of Bitcoin Classic is Bitcoin Gold. Bitcoin Gold differs from the classic in two important ways. They are branding their self as a version of Bitcoin instead of a new platform derived from Bitcoin's source code. They also kept the original Bitcoin's transaction history, which means that if you have Bitcoins before this fork, you now have the same amount of 'gold' bitcoins.

Bitcoin Gold's goal is to improve the flaw in the increasing centralization of the mining industry that secures and verifies all the transactions. Bitcoin Gold was to get rid of mining companies by introducing an alternative mining algorithm that makes it harder for people to optimize. This should allow the ordinary user to earn some cash with their spare computing cycles, just like the original Bitcoin in its early days.

Bitcoin Gold is nearly identical, in many aspects, to the original Bitcoin, but it uses a different proof-of-work algorithm known as Equihash. The supporters believe it to be impervious to being sped up with custom hardware.

Ethereum ETH

This is a public platform that takes distributed computing to a whole new level. It acts as a giant consensus machine instead of a database. Its computations are turing-complete, which means it can calculate whatever other computers can calculate, just a bit slower. Ethereum's genesis was started in July of

2015. It is the leading platform for permissionless smart contracts.

Ethereum's goal is to use blockchain to replace internet third parties, those that keep track of complex financial instruments, store data, and transfer mortgages.

There are several differences between Ethereum and Bitcoin; the biggest distinction is their capability and purpose. Ethereum's blockchain focuses on running the code for any decentralized application.

In the blockchain, miners work to earn Ether, instead of mining for bitcoin. Ether is the type of token that fuels the network. Ether, besides being a cryptocurrency, is used by app developers to purchase services and pay transaction fees on the Ethereum network.

Ethereum also has what they call smart contracts. A smart contract is a computer code that helps to facilitate the exchange of shares, property, content, money, or anything valuable. On the blockchain, a smart contract becomes similar to a self-operating computer program that will automatically execute when certain conditions have been met.

While all blockchains can process code, most are limited. Ethereum works differently. Instead of giving a set of limited operations, Ethereum lets their developers make whatever type of operations they want. This means the developers can make thousands of different applications that go past anything we have ever seen.

Ethereum gives developers the opportunity to build and deploy decentralized applications. All services that are centralized can be changed to decentralized with the use of Ethereum. Think for a moment about all of the intermediary services that live across hundreds of industries. You have the obvious service such as loans provided by banks to intermediary services rarely thought of by most such as regulatory compliance, registries, voting systems, and much more.

Use the like below to buy $100 worth of coin and receive $10 free.

https://www.coinbase.com/join/582759ff21649a5de502ef18

Ripple XRP

Ripple is in-between a public and private platform. They rely on validating nodes that are controlled by Ripple, Inc. They hope to dematerialize currencies and assets. Customers give actual assets to guardians that are called ripple gateways. These gateways then give the customer a token of these assets. This is similar to how goldsmiths used to issue receipts for gold deposits. These tokens are then sent to anyone who has a Ripple account. These can be traded for other tokens and then redeemed by giving the token back to the guardian for the actual asset.

Ripple works as a payment network, RippleNet, and a cryptocurrency, Ripple XRP, and was created in 2012. RippleNet connects to banks and other institutions and allows them to transfer assets and money through their network. Every transaction is recorded in the XRP Ledger.

The currency used for payment in the network is Ripple XRP, which reduces the money and time that can happen with cross-border payments. Every transaction in their system is processed in as little as four seconds. Ethereum takes around two minutes, whereas Bitcoin takes over an hour, while traditional systems will take around three to five days.

Their currency is also scalable; it can handle 1500 transaction each second. Their transaction fees are low. Due to these benefits, this system has already started to be used by over 75 financial institutions around the world.

Bitcoin may be a new way to make payments and bypass banks and other financial institutions. But Ripple is working with the banks to enable them with faster cross-border payments and lower fees. Others view Ripple as being against what other cryptocurrencies are supposed to stand for, this is the reason why many do not like the normal.

Some people do not like Ripple XRP because it is not a decentralized network like other types of currencies. The company had all the coins created before they launched and they still own over half of the supply.

Dashcoin DASH

Based on the Bitcoin software, Dashcoin is a next-generation digital currency. Dashcoin has been able to solve a lot of the problems that are inherent in Bitcoin by speeding up transactions, developing a decentralized governance, offering enhanced financial privacy, and funding system.

Dashcoin utilizes a two-tier network. Their first tier works the same way as Bitcoin: miners locate blocks and post a transaction to a blockchain. Their second tier, made up of servers known as Masternodes, enables extra features like budgeting, decentralized governance, private transactions, and instant transactions.

Anybody can run a Masternode, but to run one, they have to prove they own 1000 DASH. This is supposed to help against 'Sybil attacks.' The 1000 DASH are not consumed or locked, an owner of a Masternode can spend that 1000 DASH anytime they want, but doing so will cause their Masternode to turn off. Masternodes are normally hosted on virtual private servers that are run by companies like Vultr, Microsoft Azure, Amazon Web Services, and others.

There is an incentive to run a Masternode as well. You will get a portion of the reward whenever a miner finds a new block – 45% to the Masternode, 45% to the miner, and 10% is used to fund Dash-related projects through a decentralized budget system. The ROI is, at the moment, about 15%.

Litecoin LTC

Litecoin is a peer-to-peer cryptocurrency that is often called the little brother of bitcoin. It has started to gain fairly widespread adoption ever since it was started back in 2011. Litecoin is often used to transfer funds between businesses or individuals without the need for a middleman like a bank or processing service.

As compared to Bitcoin, Litecoin has improved market cap, number of coins, and speed. Litecoin is based on the same type of open source code as Bitcoin, but with some differences. Created by Charlie Lee, engineer, it was to be the silver to Bitcoin's gold. The biggest difference lies in their speed.

They can create blocks four times faster, and it can confirm the legitimacy of the transactions faster. They can also process a higher number of them during the same time frame.

Cryptocurrencies hold intrinsic value because of their limited supply. After a certain amount of coins have been created, that is all. They cannot make any more coins. For litecoin, that max number is 84 million.

They also use a different hashing algorithm for solving a block. Once a transaction has been made, it is grouped with others that have been submitted within one of the protected blocks. The miners will use their CPU or GPU cycles to figure out complex math problems and pass the data within a block through the algorithm until they discover a solution. At this point, all transactions in the blocks are completely verified and stamped as legitimate.

Miners also reap benefits every time a block is solved because a predefined number of coins are sent out to those that helped. The more powerful hashers get the lion's share.

Use the like below to buy $100 worth of coin and receive $10 free.

https://www.coinbase.com/join/582759ff21649a5de502ef18

Monero XMR

The first implementation of CryptoNote, Bytecoin, was launched in July of 2012. CryptoNote works as the application layer protocol behind several decentralized currencies.

People started to notice that some unstable things were happening and that around 80% of their coins had already been published, so they figured out the blockchain for bytecoin would fork, and all of the new coins within this new chain would be called Bitmonero. This name eventually was shortened to Monero, which means coin in Esperanto. Within a new chain, a block is mined and added every two minutes.

With Monero, your currency is yours. The miners have complete control over their transactions. They have full responsibility for their money. Since your identity is private, nobody can see what you spend your money on.

Monero is also fungible. Investopedia says the definition of fungibility as: "Fungibility is a good or asset's interchangeability with other individual goods or assets of the same type." So what exactly does that mean? Let us say you borrow $20, you can return the money with a different $20 bill, and they will not care. In fact, you could even choose to give them a $10 bill and two $5 bills. The dollar is fungible. However, if you instead borrowed their car and you come back and give them a different car, then they are going to be pretty upset with you, are nonfungible.

Bitcoin is not fungible, whereas Monero is. All of Monero's data and transactions are private, which means nobody knows what your Monero has been through, nor do they know what you have used the Monero for. Since the history of transactions is not known, it means that there is no transaction trail. This means that there are not any 'tainted' or 'clean' Monero.

IOTA MIOTA

Dr. Serguei Popov, Dominik Schiener, Sergey Ivancheglo, and David Sonstebo founded IOTA in 2015. They created a fixed supply of 2,779,530,283,277,761 Iota. There is not any mining, so no more will be created.

They work as an open-source distributed ledger that is focused on providing people with safe payments and communications between machines on the Internet of Things. They make use of DAG, directed acyclic graph, instead of the regular blockchain. Their transactions are free regardless of how big the transactions are. Their confirmation time is faster, and the number of transactions that their system can handle at one time is unlimited.

For a user to send a transaction, they also have to validate two, randomly selected, transactions. A transaction that has been sent out has to accumulate a sufficient level of verification in order for it to be 'confirmed' by the recipient.

IOTA works with one administrator known as the coordinator, who works to confirm all of the transactions in a set of released milestones. Without the use of the coordinator, the IOTA DAG is not seen as sufficiently secured in its early stages. The coordinator is supposed to be removed once their network has become a sufficient size.

ZCash ZEC

ZCash is an open-source and decentralized cryptocurrency. It defines itself as: "If Bitcoin is like HTTP for money, ZCash is https." ZCash provides its users with selective transparency and privacy of their transactions. Like https, ZCash claims it provides extra privacy or security where every transaction is published and recorded on a blockchain, but the information of the amount, sender, and recipient stay private.

ZCash gives its users the option of 'shielded' transactions, which encrypts their content using an advanced cryptographic technique known as zk-SNARK. This works to ensure the validity of all transactions and a secure ledger of balances without providing any information.

17 investors provided the Zcash Electric Coin Company with $2 million in the early months of 2016 in exchange for equity in the company. 16.4% of the company is now owned by investors. The Founders' Reward is 10% of the total monetary base of 21 million coins with the rest of the 90% going to the miners.

ZCoin XZC

The ZCoin, or Zerocoin, cryptocurrency was proposed by Johns Hopkins University graduate students Christina Garman and Ian Miers and Professor Matthew D. Green as a new extension to the bitcoin protocol that would add anonymity to transactions.

ZCoin first went live on September 28, 2016. ZCoin implemented a private instant verified transaction, known as PIVX, a proof of stake cryptocurrency.

The way the Zcoin network works is a bit technical, but the basic gist is that it involves two independent cryptographic transaction phases: the mint phase and the spending phase.

ZCoin allows its users to mint coins and then spend those coins. The separation of the two different processes ensures that minted coins cannot easily be associated with its expenditure.

Neo

The neo cryptocurrency uses a delegated byzantine fault-tolerant algorithm, DBFT. This works as a consensus mechanism, instead of proof of work or stake that gives the system the ability to resist the Byzantine general problem and keeps consensus even if a node bares malicious intentions.

The NeoX system creates the ability to execute and operate across several different blockchains. They also have their own system for smart contracts known as Neo contract. It is a mechanism to create a contract in a seamless, scalable, high-performance environment that integrates all pre-existing codebases.

NeoFS is decentralized storage service of Neo and works as a peer-to-peer Dropbox. Lastly, Neo uses NeoQ, which is a lattice-based cryptographic mechanism that makes problems that are unsolvable by quantum computers and ensures that they are quantum-proof.

Factom FCT

Factom is a usable blockchain technology that helps solve business problems by giving an unchangeable record system. They created a data layer over the bitcoin blockchain, which makes their distributed ledger technology secure. Governments and businesses can use Factom to keep track of their information so that it cannot be backdated, modified, or deleted. Their technology decentralizes record keeping by making sure the integrity of the data remains intact, providing total transparency, while also maintaining user privacy.

The decentralized distributed protocol of Factom runs on top of bitcoin. This means that it is not controlled by anybody. It is software that people around the world run to make it work. It is open source, and anybody can use it for any purpose.

Unlike most databases, Factom's blockchain is distributed over the internet, making it almost impossible to shut down. The bitcoin blockchain works as a record of financial transactions, Factom works to store any type of data. This means that Factom is an ideal platform for a large number of applications, such as legal applications, property titles, voting systems, supply chain management, medical records, financial systems, and more.

Dogecoin DOGE

Dogecoin was first introduced as a joke currency on December 6, 2013, it quickly developed an online community and in January 2014 reached a capitalization of $60 million. Its capitalization is $308 million as of December 2017.

Dogecoin had a fast initial coin production schedule: by mid-2015 100 billion coins were in circulation, with 5.256 billion coins added every year thereafter. By June 30, 2015, the 100 billionth coin had been mined.

The block time for Dogecoin is a minute. The original implementation of the Dogecoin planned for there to be a fixed amount of coins per block from block 600,001 forwards; the algorithm was changed starting with the 145,000th block so that there was always a fixed reward.

Unlike other deflationary cryptocurrencies, such as Bitcoin, there is not a limit to the number of Dogecoins that can be produced. This means that Dogecoin can compete with other inflationary coins. By February 2015, 98 billion coins had been released, with block 600,000 mined on February 25th.

Approximately 5.256 billion coins will be created each year in perpetuity. This means it has an inflation rate of 5.256% that will decay after a while because of the new coins being introduced. It is figured that the inflation rate will be around 3.4% by 2025.

Future of Cryptocurrencies

This Chapter Will Cover:

- How cryptocurrencies may fair
- If investing is a good option

Many of the limitations that many cryptocurrencies have to deal with is like the fact that your digital fortune can disappear with the crash of a computer, or that a hacker can ransack your virtual vault, could be overcome in time with advances in technology. What is going to be harder to overcome is all the inconsistency that torments cryptocurrencies; the more they grow in popularity, the more government scrutiny and regulation they will attract. This will end up eroding the fundamentals of their existence.

While the amount of businesses that will accept cryptocurrencies has continued to increase, they are still in the minority. For cryptocurrencies to be widely used, they will need to gain complete acceptance with consumers. Their complexity, when compared to traditional currencies, will probably deter a lot of people, except for those that are technologically adept.

A cryptocurrency that wants to be part of the mainstream system will likely have to satisfy a large array of criteria. It has to be mathematically complex, so to keep out hackers and fraud, but easy enough so consumers can understand them, decentralized but have adequate protection and safeguards, and preserves anonymity without being an outlet for money laundering, tax evasion, and other underhanded activities.

Since these are daunting criteria to cover, is there a chance that the top cryptocurrency in the next few years will have attributes that fall between today's cryptocurrencies and heavily-regulated fiat currencies? While the chance of this looks like it will never happen, there is no doubt that Bitcoin's success in facing their challenges might determine the fortunes of all other cryptocurrencies in the future.

Is Investing an Option?

If you are thinking about investing in cryptocurrencies, it is best for you to treat this investment the same way you treat all other ventures. Basically, recognize the fact that you could lose the biggest part of your investment, if not all of your investment.

Cryptocurrencies do not have an actual value except to the buyer who is willing to pay for it at the point of purchase. This means it is susceptible to price swings, which will increase the risk of loss for investors. For example, Bitcoin plunged from $260 to around $130 within only six hours on April 11, 2013.

If you are not able to handle that kind of volatility, look to other investments that will suit you better. While opinion continues to stay divided on Bitcoin's merits as an investment, supporters look towards its limited supply and growing use as value drivers, while people against Bitcoin view it as just another bubble. This is a debate that a conservative investor should stay away from.

A huge debate has emerged with the creation of Bitcoin and other cryptocurrencies about their future. Despite some of the recent issues Bitcoin has gone through, its success since its beginning in 2009 has inspired the creation of other cryptocurrencies like MintChip, Litecoin, and Ripple.

Any cryptocurrency that is looking to be a part of the main financial system is going to have to satisfy a large number of criteria. Even though this may appear small, there is very little doubt that Bitcoin's failure or success in handling challenges they face will determine the fortune of other types of cryptocurrencies in the future.

Conclusion

Thank you for making it through to the end of *Cryptocurrency: Understanding Bitcoin, Bitcoin Cash, Ethereum & Altcoins*. I am sure you found it informative and it was able to provide you with all of the tools you need to achieve your goals.

You have learned all the basics about many different cryptocurrencies throughout this book. You now know enough to make an informed decision on how you would like to use cryptocurrencies. They are a growing trend, and will likely keep growing in popularity. They are a pretty good investment opportunity and a great alternative to regular currency.

However, though, you must remember that the future of cryptocurrency remains untold. We never know if it will continue to shine brightly or will it be a temporary sunshine for everybody. But we can be confident that it holds a bright future especially with all the popularity and improvements it has gained today. In fact, thousands of people all around the world are trusting cryptocurrency.

We never know, but soon, we may find ourselves using cryptocurrency on a daily basis. We will find an advance economic system with the evolved finance industry. Yes, cryptocurrency is really changing the world.

Continue to study the ins and outs of cryptocurrencies. Continue to learn the problems and issues that may come up so to help yourself avoid such downfalls.

Get started today using cryptocurrencies.

Finally, if you found this book useful in any way, a review is always appreciated!

You May Also Enjoy the Following Titles from Cryptomasher

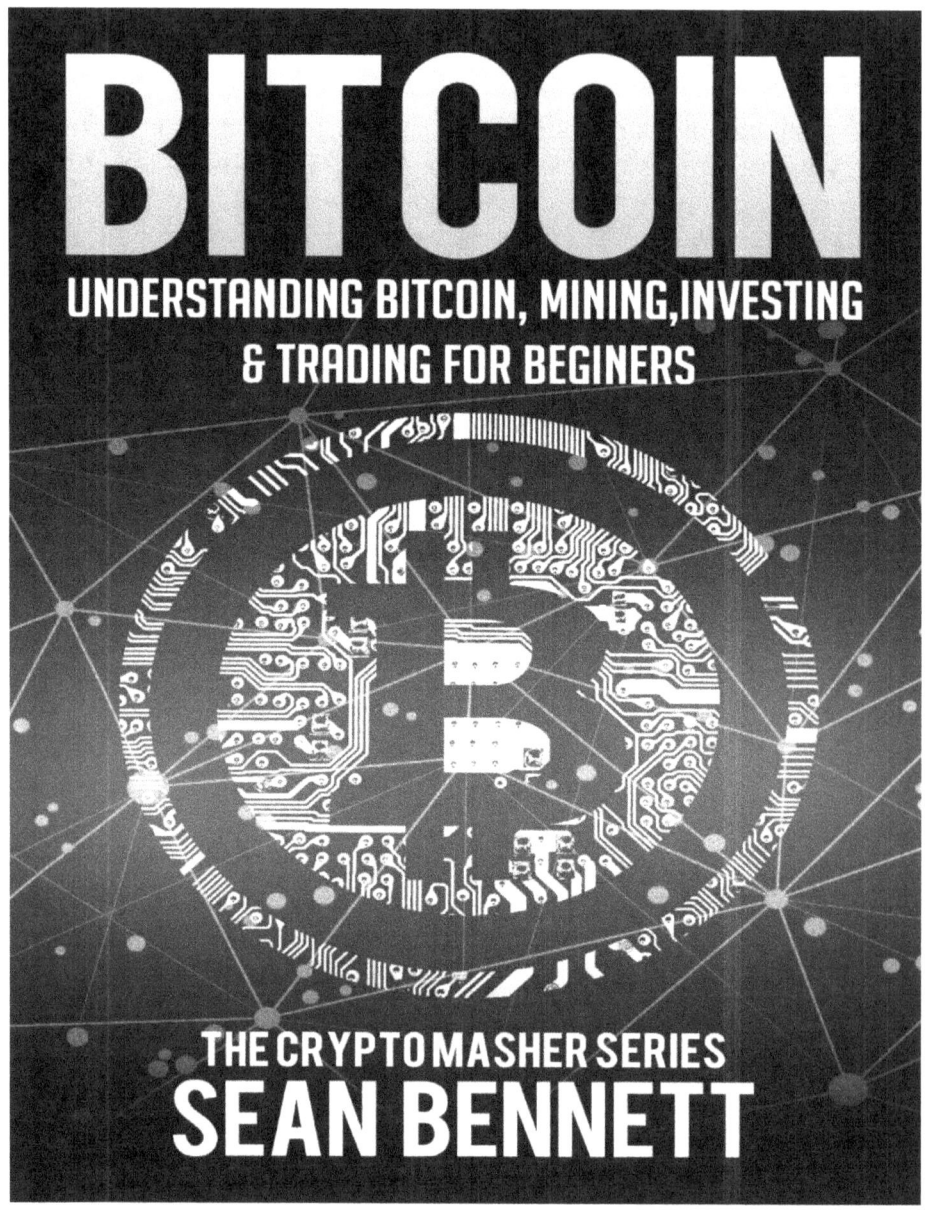

BITCOIN

UNDERSTANDING BITCOIN, MINING, INVESTING & TRADING FOR BEGINERS

THE CRYPTO MASHER SERIES
SEAN BENNETT

BLOCKCHAIN

A GUIDE TO UNDERSTANDING BLOCKCHAIN

THE CRYPTO MASHER SERIES
SEAN BENNETT

FREE eBook Available
This is my FREE GIFT to YOU

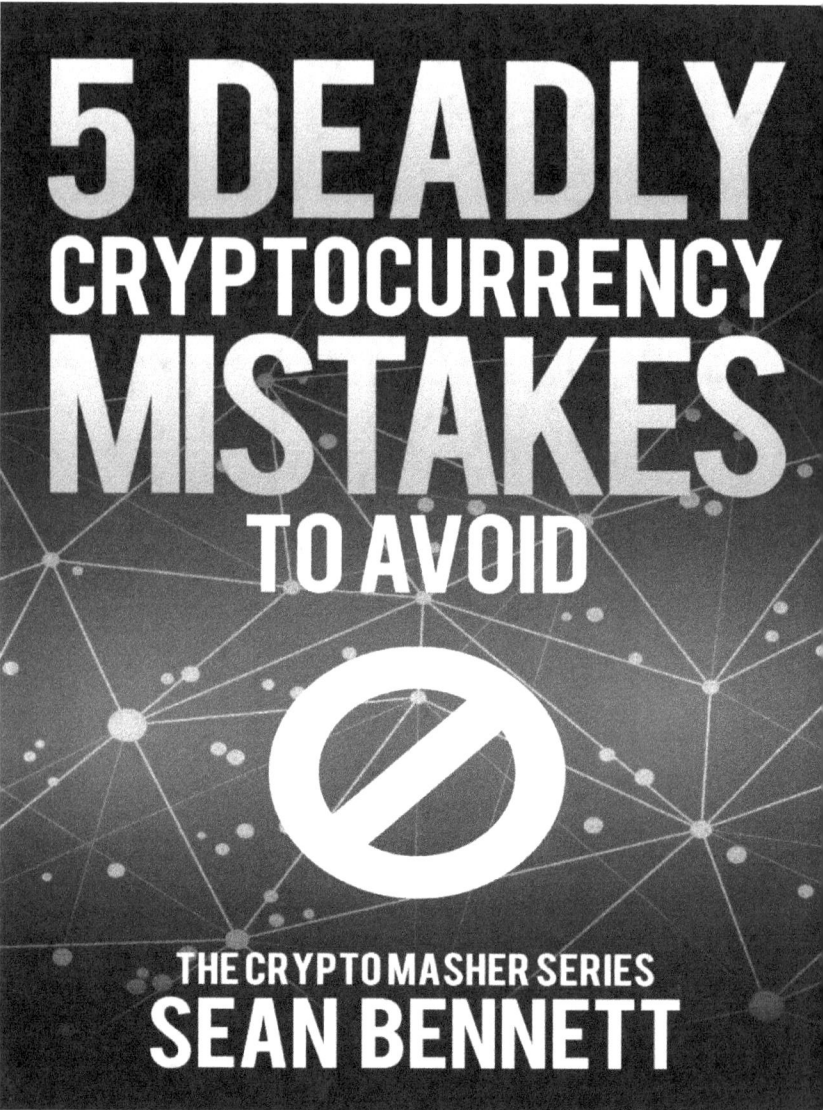

Click on the link below to collect your
FREE GIFT & Avoid the 5 Deadly
Mistakes

http://eepurl.com/c9Lsr9

www.ingramcontent.com/pod-product-compliance
Lightning Source LLC
Chambersburg PA
CBHW071232220526